Survive at Sea

Silver Dolphin
San Diego, California

Silver Dolphin Books
An imprint of the Advantage Publishers Group
5880 Oberlin Drive, San Diego, CA 92121-4794
www.silverdolphinbooks.com

WARNING!

This book provides useful information for difficult situations an individual may encounter, but it cannot guarantee results, nor can the publisher accept any responsibility for any injuries, damages, or loss resulting from the information within this book. The red WARNING symbol shown above denotes situations or activities that require caution. Never put yourself in danger and always seek the advice of an adult before trying any of the activities in this book, especially those highlighted with a WARNING symbol.

Created and produced by
Andromeda Children's Books
An imprint of Pinwheel Ltd
Winchester House, 259-269 Old Marylebone Road, London, NW1 5XJ, UK
www.pinwheel.co.uk

Copyright © 2005 Andromeda Children's Books

ISBN 1-59223-291-4

Made in China

1 2 3 4 5   09 08 07 06 05

Author Claire Llewellyn
Managing Editor Ruth Hooper, **Series Editor** Deborah Murrell
Assistant Editor Emily Hawkins
Art Director Ali Scrivens, **Art Editor** Julia Harris, **Designer** Miranda Kennedy
Production Clive Sparling
Illustrator Peter Bull
Consultant John Marriott

Contents

Introduction

You have been cast adrift on the open sea!
All you have with you is a backpack
with a few useful things inside.
It is 12 days before help can arrive.

Can you survive on your own?

Can you find fresh water and food?

Can you reach land?

Can you make use of the
things in your backpack?

Here is the survival challenge!

On each page of this book, you face a different challenge.
The 12 challenges explore every aspect of life as a
castaway—from keeping yourself safe and protecting
yourself from the elements to making your way toward
land and signaling for rescue. To meet each challenge, you
need to use your wits, the information provided, and the
equipment in your backpack. Learn to survive the challenges
and you should be able to keep going as long as you need
to. Once you have been rescued, try the quiz at the back
of the book to test your new survival skills.

What's in your backpack

blanket

plastic bags

plastic sheeting

rope   stick

candy   cup

plastic bottles   vinegar   oil

aluminum foil

bucket

woolly hat   whistle   string   bowl   sponge

bandanna

binoculars   cardboard box

camera

antiseptic cream

sea-
sickness
pills

aloe vera cream   first-aid kit

backpack

Can you get into

DAY 1 the life raft?

You are alone at sea in a boat that is damaged and sinking. You have only a few minutes to get off the boat and try to get into a life raft. Can you think clearly and save yourself?

Today's survival tools:
These things will be useful. Can you figure out how?

Your pack

plastic bottles

seasickness pills

plastic bags

bucket

In the water

Q and A

Q: Should I hang onto the damaged boat?

A: Swim or paddle away from the boat. A large boat could suck you under as it sinks.

Q: Should I take my clothes off?

A: Keep your clothes on: you'll need them later.

Q: What about my shoes?

A: Keep your shoes on—they will protect your feet. But kick off boots that could fill with water.

Q: Can a plastic bag help me float?

A: You can make a temporary float by filling a plastic bag with air. See the opposite page for instructions on how to do this.

What should you do before leaving the boat?

Try to keep a cool head. Some of the things you do now could make the difference between life and death in the days ahead. Throw the life raft into the water and wait for it to inflate. Put on warm clothing and a life jacket and grab food, water, seasickness pills, empty bottles and buckets, and anything else that might be useful. Try to board the life raft without getting wet. If you have to jump into the water, be sure to cover your nose and mouth and keep your feet together.

How can you keep afloat?

If you had time to put it on, your life jacket will help to keep you afloat. Also, salt water is easier to float in than fresh water. If you are not wearing a life jacket, tread water while you look around for anything you could use as a float. Could you hold onto empty plastic bottles? Do you have any plastic bags that you could inflate?

How can you save energy?

Although you are in danger, try to stay calm. Fear will exhaust you and make you breathe quickly and swallow water. Stop swimming for a moment and float on your back to save energy. Now take a few deep, slow breaths—you will become more relaxed and buoyant.

Can you board the life raft?

It is vital that you swim over to the life raft before you get too cold and exhausted. The body loses heat 20 times faster in water than it does in air. When you reach the life raft, grab one of the handholds. Rest a moment to get your breath and then pull yourself in.

Make a float

Try it at home!

1. Grasp an empty plastic bag by the handles. Sweep it downward to fill it with air, then tie the handles together tightly.

2. Time how long the bag stays inflated.

This time could be vital in a survival situation.

Can you protect yourself?

Well done! You have survived the wreck and managed to get yourself into the life raft. Your chances of survival are already much greater. Now you need to find a way to get warm and protect yourself from the cold and wind.

Today's survival tools:
These things will be useful.
Can you figure out how?

Your pack

sponge

plastic bags

woolly hat

oil

aluminum foil

plastic sheeting

bucket

candy

rope

Can you get warm?

If you're wet, you're at risk of hypothermia, a dangerous condition in which the body's temperature sinks below 95°F. Remove wet clothes and wrap yourself in a dry blanket, which you will find in the life raft. Wear your hat, since up to 60 percent of your body's heat can be lost through your head. Some extra blood sugar will be useful, so eat any candy you may have.

Hypothermia   Tips

Watch out for these symptoms of hypothermia:
- Goose bumps
- Violent shivering
- Pale skin that feels numb
- Feeling sluggish or drowsy
- Uncoordinated movement

Can you set up a shelter?

You are going to need a shelter to keep out the wind, rain, sun, and sea. If your life raft has a cover, close it to protect yourself from the weather. If there is no cover, you could rig one up. There may be a sheet or sail you can use. You could tie it to the handles or ropes around the edges of the raft by using the rope or string.

Can you stay warm?

Staying dry is the key to staying warm. Keep the raft as dry as you can. Dry your clothes during the day so that they keep you warm at night, when it may be very cold. Store dry things in a plastic bag. If you have some, wrap a sheet of aluminum foil around your body to help retain heat.

In the life raft

Q: How do I keep the raft dry?

A: Bail and sponge as much water out of the raft as you can.

Q: I'm feeling chilly and stiff. What can I do?

A: Do as much exercise as you can, but be careful not to capsize the raft!

Q: How can I keep from feeling sick?

A: Focus on a fixed point to stabilize yourself. This should help you feel less sick.

Can you stay dry?

If rainwater collects in the raft, it will be difficult to keep your feet dry and warm. Use a sponge to remove any excess water, but keep the water in a container, such as a bucket, in case you need it later.

Test the warming properties of aluminum foil

Try it at home!

1. Unroll 1 foot of aluminum foil.

2. Being careful with sharp edges, wrap the foil around one of your arms.

3. Leave it on for a minute or two. Can you feel the difference?

How can you protect your skin from salt?

Skin often becomes sore at sea because of the salty water, which can cause rashes, boils, and sores. Always wear clothes to protect your skin, and keep as dry as you can. Rinse your skin with rainwater and keep it well oiled to prevent it from cracking.

Will you be safe
in your raft?

Now you are feeling better. Your next challenge is to make your raft safe in choppy seas and stow all your belongings carefully. Try not to worry about your situation. Think clearly and positively—after all, you could still be in the water!

Today's survival tools:
These things will be useful. Can you figure out how?

Your pack

string

first-aid kit with bandages and safety pins

rope

Can you fix leaks in the life raft?

Your raft is your new home. Treat it with care and check it regularly for signs of wear. If you find any weak areas, reinforce them to prevent punctures. Use the puncture kit that comes with the raft to do this. For small areas, you could use bandages. If it is hot during the day, the air in the raft will expand and put extra pressure on the seams. Let out a little air to reduce the pressure. At night, when it is cold, you can top up the air again.

Protecting your raft

Q and A

Q: How long should the life raft last?

A: Life rafts are built to last approximately 30 days.

Q: Where is the raft most likely to wear and need repairing?

A: The raft is most likely to wear on the sides, where ropes rub against it. Pad these places with something soft, such as clothing or blankets if you have spares.

Q: Help! The repair patches will not stick on the wet raft.

A: Stuff the hole with something solid. Try to use the patch again later, when the area is dry.

Can you stop drifting?

You want to stay near your boat's wreckage in case someone comes to rescue you—but the current is carrying your raft away. Tie the sea anchor that comes with the raft to the back of it with a long rope. As it sinks, it works like an ordinary anchor to prevent drifting. It will also help keep the raft from capsizing.

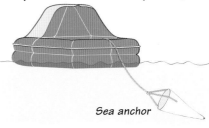

Sea anchor

What supplies do you have on the raft?

Now that you and your raft are safe, it is time to check what there is on the life raft and what supplies you have brought on board. Safeguard every item by putting it inside the raft's pockets or tying it down securely. Attach the most valuable small items to your clothing with safety pins to make them doubly secure. If you have a lot of supplies on board, you can save space inside by using rope or string to tie waterproof items to the handholds on the outside.

Practice tying a figure-eight knot

Try it at home!

1. Wrap a rope one and a half times around a post so that both ends are pointing in the same direction.

2. Pass the right end of the rope under the left.

3. Now pass the short end over the long end and up through the loop.

A figure-eight knot will hold tight and not slip. It's safe and simple to tie.

11

Can you find fresh water?

DAY 4

Your raft and equipment are secure. You may have some water stored in the raft. However, at sea you are exposed to the sun and wind, and risk becoming dehydrated. To prevent this, you need to find some clean water to drink.

USE CAUTION

Today's survival tools:

These things will be useful. Can you figure out how?

Your pack

sponge

cup

plastic sheeting

bowl

Can you drink seawater?

You might think that being in the ocean surrounded by water means dehydration will not be a problem. However, seawater is much too salty to drink and would be very harmful. In the short term, it would make you sick, dehydrating your body even more. In the long term, it could seriously damage your kidneys. Do not drink it!

Rainfall

Tips

1. Don't wait for the rain before setting up collectors—be prepared!

2. Keep your rainwater collectors set up at night while you sleep.

3. Some rain will fall in your raft. Collect every drop with a clean sponge and squeeze it into a bowl to use as nondrinking water.

4. Think of the rain as a shower—use it to clean yourself.

What if you run short of water?

If you are very short of water, you will need to ration supplies. Drink as little as possible while you look for a fresh supply. Eat as little as possible, because your body uses water to digest food. Don't worry about this: you can survive for up to a month without food. However, you can only survive for about a week without water!

Can you make fresh water from seawater?

You may find that your life raft came with a solar still, but if not, you can always make your own (see below). This will not produce a huge amount of water, but it will keep you going. Also, because the water is distilled, it is as safe to drink as rainwater.

How a solar still works

A solar still uses the warmth of the sun to evaporate the seawater. This produces water vapor, which rises into the air, leaving the salt behind. When the water vapor cools again, it forms droplets of pure, fresh water on the plastic sheet. These droplets slide down and fall into the cup in the center.

How can you reduce water loss?

Keeping your skin covered and staying out of the sun and wind helps reduce water loss. Dampen your clothes with seawater to keep cool without the need for sweating. Breathing through your nose instead of your mouth also helps retain moisture.

Try it at home!

Make a solar still

1. Put salty water about an inch deep in a large bowl with an empty cup in the center.

2. Drape a plastic sheet or bag over the bowl and secure it at the edges with heavy objects.

3. Put a heavy object in the middle so that the plastic sheet forms a cone over the cup.

4. Fresh water will condense on the underside of the plastic and drip into the cup.

What will you find to eat?

Your survival rations are getting low, so today's challenge is to find some food. There are many different kinds of food in the sea, but how do you go about getting to it? And can you eat it uncooked?

USE CAUTION

Today's survival tools:
These things will be useful. Can you figure out how?

Your pack

aluminum foil

bucket　　string

first-aid kit with safety pins

What is the easiest food to find?

Depending on which ocean you are in, you may find the easiest food to find is seaweed, which can be found floating on the surface all around you. Seaweed is full of vitamins and minerals, but is also very salty and hard to digest raw. This means that you should not eat seaweed unless you have a plentiful supply of fresh water. If you do decide to eat it, choose only seaweed that is firm to the touch and does not have an odor.

Can you catch and eat fish?

Tiny fish are swimming around the raft. Can you scoop them up in a bucket? You may even find that flying fish leap into the raft by themselves! Fish are high in protein, but, like seaweed, you should only eat them if you have enough fresh water to drink. Also, you will not be able to cook the fish you catch, and you may not like the idea of eating them raw.

Can you make a fishing line?

You can make a simple fishing line out of a piece of string with an open safety pin tied to the end. To get a bite, you'll need some bait. Try using tiny fish, which you could scoop up in a bucket or other container, and add something shiny, like foil, to make a lure. Night is a great time for fishing and fish are attracted to light. The moonlight will reflect off the foil in the water and attract fish.

Seafood

Q: Can I eat the shrimp on the seaweed I've found?

A: Shrimp are edible, but you will have to eat them raw!

Q: Are all parts of a fish safe to eat?

A: It's not always safe to eat the internal organs of fish, since some can contain poisons.

Q: Can you eat plankton?

A: Yes. Plankton is a mass of tiny plants and animals that floats on the ocean's surface.

Safe fish

- Bass
- Mullet
- Grouper
- Skate
- Mackerel

Dangerous fish

- Porcupine fish
- Stingray
- Stonefish
- Triggerfish
- Weaver fish

Which fish are safe to eat?

As a general rule, it is safer to eat fish that live offshore than those that live close to land. However, many fish have stingers, barbs, or sharp spines, and it is best to avoid these! There are also many poisonous fish to watch out for. They are often brightly colored, so they are easy to spot. See the lists at left for examples of some that are safe to eat and some that are not.

Can you sail the raft?

Five days have passed since your boat went down. You've been hoping someone would come to rescue you, but no one has appeared. Now it's time to pull up the sea anchor and look for land.

Why look for land?

There is little chance of being rescued now. With no radio, you have no way of seeking help. If your raft came with flares, they will only be useful if you see a boat or a plane to signal to. You remember seeing some islands to the north. It might be worth trying to reach them. It would certainly be easier to survive on land than to survive at sea.

Today's survival tools:

Your pack

These things will be useful. Can you figure out how?

rope

string

Will the wind help?

At the moment, you are drifting with the wind and current. Rafts cannot sail against the wind. If the wind or current is against you, you can't do anything about it. Luckily, both the wind and the current are in your favor at the moment, and will take you in the direction of the islands you spotted earlier.

16

Can you harness the wind?

When the wind is blowing in the right direction, you can use your life raft's cover as a sail. Turn the raft so that the wind blows straight into the canopy (the wind will probably help you to do this). Now the wind will help you reach your destination.

The life raft's cover makes a good sail.

Can you steer the raft?

When you get closer to land, you may find obstacles, such as rocks, which you'll need to steer around to get to the shore. There may also be coral reefs below the surface of the water. These would damage the underside of the raft, so you want to avoid them. You need a rudder to steer the raft properly. Using rope or string, fix a paddle to the handle on the back of the raft. With the paddle in the water, moving the handle to the left or right will change the raft's direction. Now you can steer your raft safely ashore!

Find north

1. In the Northern Hemisphere, find the seven-star constellation known as the **Big Dipper**.

2. The two stars furthest from the Big Dipper's "handle" always point toward the **North Star**.

3. Follow their line for about four times the distance between them and you will find the North Star.

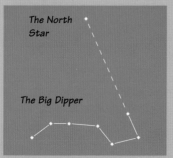

The North Star

The Big Dipper

Find south

1. In the Southern Hemisphere, find the Southern Cross. It is the smallest of three cross-shaped groups, and has two "pointer stars."

2. Follow an imaginary line along the crosspiece to the right, and four and a half times its length.

3. This point lies over the southern horizon. Try to find a landmark, such as a hill, to help you remember the spot.

Try it at home!

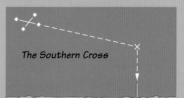

The Southern Cross

17

Can you protect yourself from the sun?

Today, the sky is clear and the temperature is soaring. Your challenge is to cope with the heat. Can you protect yourself from the sun's dangerous rays?

Today's survival tools:

Your pack

These things will be useful. Can you figure out how?

bucket

bandanna

first-aid kit with scissors

cardboard box

string

How can you keep out of the sun?

Stay in the shade under the raft's cover during the hottest part of the day. Try to arrange it so that the breeze can blow through, to keep it from getting too stifling. Use a bucket or bowl to pour seawater over the cover regularly; this will help cool everything down.

How can you cool off?

You are feeling hot and sticky. The best way to cool off would be to go for a swim! But you don't want to risk being bitten or stung. The safest thing to do is to splash your clothes with seawater. But don't soak them—you want them to dry before night falls or you will be too cold to go to sleep.

Cooling down

Q and **A**

Q: Wouldn't I be cooler if I took my clothes off?

A: Don't be tempted to take off your clothes—you will get sunburned.

Q: The sun is beating down on my head. How can I protect it?

A: Wet the bandanna and tie it around your head. Try to cover your neck as well.

Q: Should I keep my clothes wet all the time?

A: Too much salt water will make your skin sore. Also, if your clothes are not dry by dusk you will be shivering all night.

Can you avoid sunstroke?

Your head is aching and you feel a little dizzy. You may have sunstroke. This is a dangerous condition in which the body overheats. Stop whatever you are doing, rest for a while in the shade and sip fresh water slowly. It's best not to do anything at all during the hottest part of the day.

Sunstroke

Facts!

Sunstroke is caused by staying too long or working too hard in the hot sun. Early symptoms include:

- Feverishness
- Bad headache
- Dizziness
- Vomiting
- Difficulty walking

Treatment: Lie in the shade under a wet blanket. Find something to use as a fan.

How can you protect your eyes from the glare?

The sunlight on the sea is dazzling and your eyes are becoming sore. You must find a way to protect them. If you have a pair of sunglasses, wear them. If not, try making some out of cardboard (see below). You will be surprised at how well you can see through the slits, and your eyes will be protected from the glare.

Make sunglasses out of a cardboard box

Try it at home!

1. Cut a rectangle about 2 inches deep and 8 inches wide from the cardboard box.

2. Mark a middle line. Cut two 1-inch slits for your eyes and a notch for your nose.

3. Make holes and attach two strings at the ends to tie around your head.

Can you deal with sharks?

You have come face to face with a shark! You may be the target of a shark attack. Can you stay calm and collected? Can you frighten the shark away?

Today's survival tools:
These things will be useful. Can you figure out how?

Your pack

blanket   stick   rope

Shark safety (Tips)

1. Don't swim among schools of fish. Sharks are attracted to large groups of fish.

2. Don't swim at dawn or dusk, or during the night. Sharks feed most actively at these times.

3. Don't enter the water with an open wound. Sharks will smell the blood.

4. Stay out of the water when you are fishing. Sharks will be attracted to the bait.

How can you avoid attracting sharks?

Sharks have very sharp senses. They can feel movements in the water from far away. Many sharks can pick up even the faintest smells. Use this knowledge to protect yourself. If you have to enter the water, try not to splash; this can attract a shark's attention. If you spear a fish, sharks may smell the blood, so do not enter the water. If you toss inedible food into the sea, do it a little at a time.

Dangerous sharks

Bull shark
Average length:
10–12 feet
Color: gray
Habitats: temperate,
coastal ocean waters;
some freshwater
rivers and lakes

Tiger shark
Average length:
10–16 feet
Color: grayish brown
Habitat: temperate,
coastal ocean waters

Great white shark
Average length:
12–16 feet
Color: gray to blue-
gray
Habitat: temperate,
coastal ocean waters

What should you do if you see a shark?

You are swimming in the water when you suddenly spot a triangular fin. It's a shark! Try not to panic; calmly return to the raft. Swim as smoothly and as quietly as you can, using the breast stroke. Get into the raft and then keep your arms and legs away from the edge. Some sharks like to swim under rafts. If you tie something large, like a blanket or tarpaulin, behind the raft with a rope, it may help keep the shark away.

What should you do if a shark looks like it is about to attack?

Sharks are inquisitive animals. If a shark keeps its distance, then it is probably just being curious. But if it circles inward and humps its back, it may be about to attack. Grasp a stick or paddle tightly and hold it out toward the shark. If it comes toward you, hit it hard on the nose, eyes, or gills. Keep on hitting it, but try not to make too much of a commotion or you may attract other sharks.

Are there any other dangerous creatures?

There are plenty of other dangerous creatures in the ocean. Watch out for the fast, razor-toothed barracuda fish and poisonous animals like the blue-ringed octopus and sea snakes. Jellyfish are not dangerous, but they can give a nasty sting. Many fish have spines or barbs, which can deliver a painful poison if you touch them.

Shark attacks

Fewer than 100 shark attacks on humans are reported each year.

If a shark attacks a person, it's usually by mistake. The shark quickly realizes it has caught something other than its normal prey and will usually let go!

Not all triangular fins you see belong to sharks. They may be the fins of whales or dolphins, or the wing tips of a large ray.

21

Could you cope in a storm?

The clouds are gathering and the sky is dark overhead. The wind is picking up and it looks as though there will soon be heavy rain. Your challenge for today is to prepare yourself and your raft for a storm.

How can you tell when bad weather is coming?

Sailors are always looking for changes in the sky and the wind. Can you learn to predict worsening weather? Practice testing for wind direction; wet a finger and hold it above your head. The side that feels coldest is the side from which the wind is blowing. Any clouds you can see in that direction will soon be over you. Practice recognizing the various cloud types and the weather they bring. Notice changing colors in the sky and make a note of the weather that follows, so that you can be prepared the next time.

Today's survival tools:

Your pack

These things will be useful. Can you figure out how?

seasickness pills   **string**

rope

bucket

How can you prepare the raft for a storm?

Check your raft carefully and repair any damage now. Make sure everything is tied down tightly with rope or string. Double your knots—you don't want to lose any equipment. Put out the sea anchor. It will lessen the raft's movement and help keep it stable.

How can you prepare yourself?

You won't be able to collect water in the storm, so put out your bucket and other collectors and collect what you can. Take a seasickness pill so the waves won't make you feel too ill. Finally, make sure your life jacket is fastened and tie yourself to the raft with rope. Now close the raft's cover and sit in the middle to stabilize the raft. Be confident: rafts are buoyant and hard to sink. The sea may be rough, but you are unlikely to capsize.

Clouds

Tips

Different kinds of clouds bring different kinds of weather.

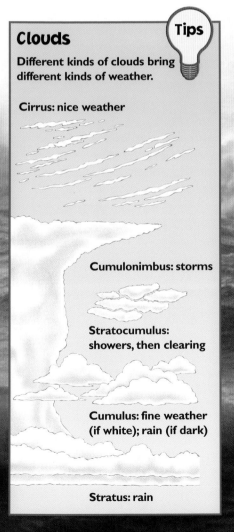

Cirrus: nice weather

Cumulonimbus: storms

Stratocumulus: showers, then clearing

Cumulus: fine weather (if white); rain (if dark)

Stratus: rain

Keep a weather diary

Try it at home!

1. Record the weather for seven days at the same time, morning and evening.

2. Observe, draw, and label the clouds. Is the weather wet or dry? Can you predict the weather by looking at the clouds?

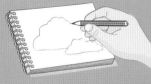

A small notebook is perfect for a weather diary.

3. Make a note of the wind direction and whether it feels light, medium, or strong.

4. Read the temperature from a thermometer.

Can you stay healthy?

The storm is over, the sea is calm, and you are sailing north again. You have seen no other boats on the ocean. What happens if you get sick or have some kind of injury? With no way of reaching a doctor, can you perform first aid?

Today's survival tools:

Your pack

These things will be useful. Can you figure out how?

first-aid kit with gauze, safety pins, and tweezers

vinegar

antiseptic cream   aloe vera gel   seasickness pills

Can you deal with seasickness?

The movement of the raft is making you nauseous. Take a seasickness pill. Seasickness is serious: it can dehydrate and exhaust you. Also, the smell of vomit is unpleasant and could attract sharks to the raft. If you are sick, wash yourself and the raft with seawater. Lie down and rest.

How to avoid seasickness

Tips

1. Don't eat if you feel sick.

2. Keep looking at the horizon. Gazing at a distant focal point can help you overcome nausea.

3. Don't keep your head in one position. Move around regularly.

4. Try a method called acupressure: press firmly on the inside of your forearms, about 2 inches up from your wrist.

First aid

Q and A

Q: I have sores on my skin. What should I do?

A: Wash the sores with fresh water and allow them to dry. Apply an antiseptic cream. Do not pick any scabs.

Q: I've cut myself. How can I stop the bleeding?

A: Press the edges of the wound together—in time it will seal. Put a soft, clean pad on the wound and wrap firmly (but not too tightly) with gauze.

How do you treat a jellyfish sting?

You have been stung by a jellyfish and your leg is burning. Quickly rinse the sting with fresh water and remove any tentacles from the skin. The tweezers in the first-aid kit will be useful for this. Next, pour vinegar over the sting—vinegar is an acid, and an antidote to the poison; it will help reduce the pain. Now, lie down in the recovery position (see below) and rest, keeping your leg still. You should do as little as possible while your body uses its energy to fight the poison. The recovery position is usually the most comfortable to lie in for long periods. You can roll onto your other side if you feel uncomfortable.

You have a bad sunburn. What should you do?

Wash the area with cool, fresh water, then dry it gently and apply aloe vera gel. Take care not to break any blisters. Make a pad out of gauze, wet it with fresh water, and press it on your burns. Keep your skin covered and stay out of the sun.

Lie in the recovery position

Try it at home!

Lie on one side. Bend your upper arm and use the back of your hand to support your head. Bend your upper leg and rest it in front of you to stabilize your body.

How should you treat a fish bite?

If you are bitten by a fish or any other sea creature, wash the wound thoroughly in clean water for about five minutes to get rid of germs. Dry the wound gently. If you have any antiseptic cream, apply some to the wound and cover it with a bandage. Change the bandage, wash the wound, and apply antiseptic cream daily to keep it clean.

How can you find land?

You have been sailing north for the past five days. Today's challenge is to find the islands you saw earlier. What signs will tell you that land is near? And, if you find the islands, can you land your life raft safely?

How do you know if land is near?

Certain signs tell you when land is near. If you spot a seal or lots of driftwood in the water, you are probably close to land. Cumulus clouds often sit over land. Seabirds often fly away from land in the morning and go back to roost in the afternoon. Follow them if you can.

What should you do if you see land?

You are scanning the horizon when you suddenly spot land. You have found an island! Try to steer the raft toward it, using your paddle rudder. Use your binoculars to examine the island carefully; try to make a mental map of everything you can see. Look for landmarks, high ground, rivers, and vegetation. These things are often much easier to see at a distance than when you are close up.

Today's survival tools:

your pack

These things will be useful. Can you figure out how?

binoculars   rope

What should you do to land your raft?

Fasten your life jacket tightly and put on your shoes. Attach yourself to the raft with the rope. Bring the sea anchor into the raft and make sure that everything is tied down securely. Between waves, paddle hard toward the beach. Try to time your landing so that you ride in on the crest of a large wave, which will take you further up the beach. Get out of the raft as soon as it is grounded and drag it inland, past the high tide line. Tie it to something solid and secure, such as a tree.

Landing the life raft

Q: When is the best time to land the raft?

A: Always land in daylight. Don't attempt to land in the dark.

Q: What if a rip current carries me out to sea?

A: A rip current is a surge of water escaping from the beach. Don't fight it. Paddle across it and head back to shore, keeping clear of the current.

Q: How do I know when to get out of the raft?

A: Jump out of the raft as soon as it has grounded. Quickly drag it above the tide line.

Sketch local landmarks

Try it at home!

1. Find a view that you would like to draw—from a window, perhaps, or a park bench.

2. Now sketch the land in front of you, labeling trees, hills, and other landmarks. Show the distances between them.

Where should you land?

Before you decide where to land, it's a good idea to paddle around the island to find the best landing place. First, examine the shore to see if there are any signs of people, who could come out and rescue you. If not, test the wind direction and paddle around to the side of the island that is sheltered from the wind. Try to find a gently sloping beach where the surf is not too strong. Stay away from coral reefs, rocks, strong surf, and cliffs.

Can you get rescued?

Congratulations! You've survived at sea for 11 days and have managed to reach dry land. Today you face your final challenge. A plane is flying over the island. Can you get the pilot to see you and come to your rescue?

How can you make the pilot see you?

When pilots are flying over land, they notice anything out of the ordinary. Good, clear signals of any kind will attract their attention. In general, the larger the signal you can make, the better chance it has of being seen. Find the highest, flattest area on the island from which to send your signal. Then decide what kind of signal will be best for the time, the place, and the weather.

Today's survival tools:

Your pack

These things will be useful. Can you figure out how?

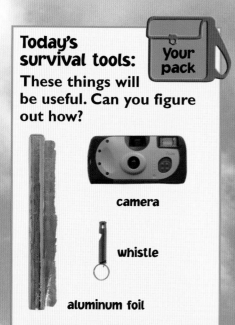

camera

whistle

aluminum foil

How can you signal on a sunny day?

On a clear day, the best way to make a signal is to reflect the sun. Smooth, shiny things make good reflectors: you could use a mirror or aluminum foil. Tilt your reflector toward the sun until light is reflected on the ground, then move the flash up toward the plane. Flash six times, then wait a minute. After the sun sets, you can use a flashlight or the flash on your camera to signal in the dark.

Rescue

Q and A

Q: How can I tell if the pilot has seen my signal?

A: The pilot will tip the plane's wings or flash a green light.

Q: How will the pilot know that I need to be rescued?

A: Use your body to signal. Face the plane with your arms raised, then wave your arms up and down.

Q: If the plane has to land far away, how will the pilot find me?

A: Blow on your whistle: the pilot will be able to track the sound.

How do you signal with flares?

USE CAUTION

Your life raft may have been equipped with flares. These will make a great signal. Choose the color of your flare carefully, so that it can be seen easily against the background. If the land around you is covered in trees and green plants, a red flare will be easiest for the pilot to see. If you are on a sandy beach, white will be difficult to see, but both red and green will show up well. Flares of all colors are useful at night. Carefully follow the instructions that come with the flares. Fire one when you hear the plane's engines, followed by a second one after a short pause. If your flares are handheld, be sure to hold them at arm's length, being careful not to get burned.

Can you write a ground-to-air message?

You can write a message using sticks or stones on the beach or on open ground. But if the pilot does not understand your language, this may not be very helpful. There are internationally recognized signals that you can use for simple messages, including:

X: "Unable to move on."

LL: "All is well."

II: "Need medical supplies."

Once you have made contact, you can answer any messages the pilot drops to you with "A" or "Y" for "Yes," or "N" for "No."

Write an international message

Try it at home!

1. With a friend, practice writing messages to each other on paper, using the international symbols.

2. Try writing "Unable to move on," using the letter "X."

3. Try writing "All is well," using the letters "LL."

4. Your friend could drop a note to you asking a question, to which you might reply with "Yes" (Y or A) or "No" (N).

X LL Y N

So you think you could survive?

How much have you learned about survival at sea? Can you answer these questions correctly? All the information can be found in the book. After taking the quiz, check your answers on page 32.

1. What should you do before you leave a sinking boat?

a. Strip down to your underwear

b. Put on warm clothing and a life jacket

c. Pack a suitcase

2. What's the best way to prevent hypothermia?

a. Sit where the wind can dry you off

b. Float in the sea

c. Remove wet clothing, wrap up, and keep out of the wind

3. Your skin is sore. What should you do?

a. Wrap it in foil

b. Rinse it with fresh water, then rub in oil and keep it covered

c. Dampen it with seawater

4. What should you do if you are short of water?

a. Stop eating and ration your fresh water

b. Drink seawater

c. Eat seaweed

5. How many times faster does your body lose heat in water than in air?

a. 10 times

b. 20 times

c. 30 times

6. Where is your life raft most likely to wear and need repairing?

a. On the top

b. Underneath

c. On the sides

7. How can you make the raft move faster?

a. By changing direction

b. By using the canopy as a sail

c. By throwing things overboard

8. Which of these can help you find north and south?

a. The stars

b. The wind

c. The currents

9. How can you protect yourself from sunstroke?

a. By wearing sunglasses

b. By taking off your clothes

c. By resting in the shade during the hottest parts of the day

10. A shark is about to attack your raft. What should you do?

a. Grab a paddle and hit it

b. Throw it some fish

c. Tie a blanket to the raft

11. You've been stung by a jellyfish. You should:

a. Wash the sting and cover it with a bandage

b. Remove any tentacles and pour vinegar on the sting

c. Leave any tentacles to drop out by themselves and rub the area with aloe vera gel

12. It's late afternoon and you see a flock of birds. What does it mean?

a. There are a lot of fish in the area

b. The birds are migrating

c. You are probably near land

13. Where is the best place to land your raft?

a. By a cliff

b. On a sloping beach

c. By a coral reef

14. Which is the best rescue signal to use at night?

a. A flare from the raft

b. A ground-to-air message

c. A reflector

Now check your answers with those on page 32. How many did you answer correctly?

12–14 correct answers:

Congratulations; you're a true survivor!

9–11 correct answers:

Pretty good; you'd probably make it through!

4–8 correct answers:

You might be lucky and survive, but you could probably do with learning some more skills!

1–3 correct answers:

Try not to get cast adrift at sea—or brush up on your survival skills first!

Index

Picture credits: All photographic images supplied by Corbis. 4–5 David Pu'u; 6–7 Martin Smith-Rodden, SYGMA; 10–11 Layne Kennedy; 12–13 Henley & Savage; 14–15 Ralph A. Clevenger; 16–17 Staffan Widstrand; 20–21 John Lund; 22–23 Lowell Georgia; 26–27 Craig Tuttle; 28–29 Paul Edmondson.

Answers to quiz on pages 30–31:

1. b, *2*. c, *3*. b, *4*. a, *5*. b, *6*. c, *7*. b, *8*. a, *9*. c, *10*. a, *11*. b, *12*. c, *13*. b, *14*. a